WAY DOWN BACK

A Journey Into Hospice Country

Caroline Macdonald

Photos courtesy of Harvey Reid

For permission to reproduce, please contact:

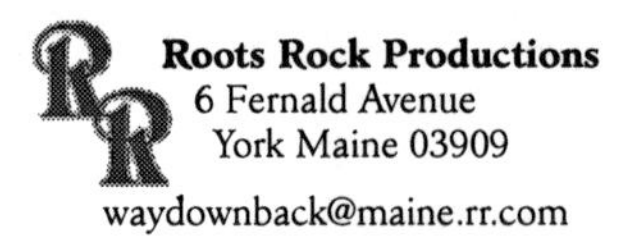

Roots Rock Productions
6 Fernald Avenue
York Maine 03909
waydownback@maine.rr.com

Set in Bembo and Minister Std.

ISBN 978-1-63029-043-6

To the patients, and the families~
the nurses, social workers,
chaplains, aides, and volunteers I have
listened to on this path.

"Poetry is really music for the human voice.

It needs to be read, it needs to be spoken.

It needs to come across the speaker's tongue to
someone's ear.

Then it comes to its real fullness."

~Maya Angelou

THE POEMS

A VETERAN'S PLEA

When You Come to Help Me Die:

I.

Just be a witness to me.
Don't startle me
or get behind me
as I sit against the wall in the back of a room.
If I choose to tell you things,
just listen and be ready to hear whatever it is I say.
You have two ears, just one mouth,
so I'd guess you can do twice as much listening as talking.
You've got to understand something:
We were trained to be wolves and we acted like wolves –
we became wolves –
I work every day to keep the wolf down –
for years I have been doing this.
It's the way I hold on to my dignity.
I ask you to allow me that.
My wife? She knows.
She knows not to try to get inside;
She takes notes at lectures, but she doesn't ask me questions.

II.

I buried the word VietNam for 13 years.
When the Wall was dedicated I broke open and wept and wept
and the rivers of sadness swept me to the delta.
We were suppose to cover each other –
a sector, a back, a life –
Bands of brothers jungled, counting on each other.
Our goal was to come home alive –
One year, we said, one year –

The bond was indelible,
but one boy from Wisconsin didn't make it;

the plan was bungled,
killed by friendly fire.

III.
I'll be riding my bike and a truck will go by.
It's the diesel; the smell of diesel
takes me back, all the way back.
I have to brake so that I don't shatter.
Who can understand this?
They have a name for it that doesn't come close to describing it.
Looking for the ties that bind, that connect, that comfort, that
take away the loneliness
of triggered memory and savagery –

Clearly I can't forget – I can't lay it aside.
Forget the medication – don't bring me the zombie potions to
alleviate my pain.
Please –
Just bring me a comrade in arms.

ADVANCED DIRECTIVES 101

I've read it in the newspapers
Seen it on the TV
There's even posters at the senior center.
They're all talking about "having the conversation," like it was the most important string of words you could ever utter.
Just thinking about "it" – "the conversation" – gets my stomach all balled up.

"Talk to your doctor," they say.
Well, I don't know about your doctor, but mine?
He doesn't ask me, he tells me and if I ask, he just tells me again.
I mean, who's talking to who is what I want to know.
Sometimes I darned well feel like telling him a thing or two, but my appointment always seems to run out of time.
The last time I was in hospital, the social work lady was hell bent on me signing a paper about the durable power and the DNR, the DNI, the DNH, the DN-THIS, the DN-THAT!
Initials and small print, do-not's and wherefores.
My heavens, you almost need a lawyer with a dictionary.
I finally said to her, "Later, my family and I will figure it out later."
She said, "Don't make later too late."

My daughter and I do think about what's going to happen when I get closer to my time.
My sons get fidgety and sharp when the subject comes up. It's not that they're nasty;
it's just hard for them to imagine their mama being old, passing on.
Maybe they talk to their sister in the other room when I'm not around and maybe they think about it more than they let on but they certainly aren't at "the conversation" stage.
I knew how to take care of my mother.
I knew she didn't want to waste away in some hallway under florescent bulbs, wrapped in tubes and fed by pumps;

she wanted to be home.
When her body told her to stop eating she did;
gently squeezed sponge water was plenty of wet.
We let her rest; she slept a lot.
I guess these days it's not enough just to tell someone.
Can't count on them remembering it straight or
being there when it counts.
Maybe that's what that woman in the hospital was getting at.
If I see her again, she can write down my list:
Pluck my chin;
Brush my hair;
Wash between my toes;
Massage my whole body with sweet oil;
And for God's sake,
Let me be.

IN EXTREMIS

Since I was nine I have been paying somehow
to get someone somewhere out of purgatory.
Every week a nickel 'n dime bet on a smooth ride.

Here I am 97 and the very thought of that tithe tethers my soul.
I wonder; is there a collection for me?
My pocket is torn and I've run out of change,
struck by fear of a broken ladder;
Heaven seems farther away than what I was led to believe.

I've had a great run.
The Army awarded me a purple heart for the blood of war.
NASA proclaimed my engineering innovations cutting edge.
My wife always smiled at my touch.
My children found my lap a safe place and still bring
their children and grandchildren by for visits.
Friends and I have shared many a stiff drink and hearty laugh.
Good soldier, good husband, good father, good citizen
getting through the hard times,
making the best of the hand that's dealt.
So what is it I don't deserve?
Do I not have the right jewels in my crown for the Pope?
I should have put more in the envelope.

I confess: over the years I raced through the mundane,
indifferent to the sacraments.
I scoffed: we were sacred but the church was scarred.
We made a full life unencumbered by the communion of saints.
Then why am I calling the priest to give me the last rites?!
I'm scared to be pulled back;
I'm more scared not to make the call.
Will he demand penance for my errant ways?
Will he grace me with absolution?

Will his words bring me peace?
When he weighs and measures my years he might find me
deficient, lacking in substance.
Maybe I haven't suffered enough.

Domine non sum dignus.
Oh Father, I beseech thee, forgive me;
Grant me the strength to leave.
Annoint me.
Love me.

BUNDLING REGRETS

Dry-eyed, lids sand-hewn overnight,
she struggled to admit to the new light of day.
Immediately, the list began;
each day, each step needed further definition.
Open eyes;
Turn head;
Look outside;
Determine.
What day is it? What time is it?
Which foot first?
Would it be a good day or one to ward off demons?

Bothersome memories made for scratchy skin, dull dread in the heart and the phantasmagoria of the might-have-been.
On a good day it was almost possible to let them go, to believe that it was too late to sort out the whys and wherefores of the Duty sex, the Survival lies, the Peacekeeping half-truths.
After all, what good does it do to ruminate on days passed?
Oh for god's sake! Cows ruminate!
Cud – was that what her life had turned into? Cud?
To be constantly regurgitated and gummed again and again?

While mouthing the serenity prayer *ad nauseum*,
her daughter had told her to stop perseverating,
getting trapped, rutted; as if the constant application of a lavender lotion removed age spots.
Was it now necessary to be a support group of one
just to get through a day?
If only she had known the meaning of "red flags" –
If only someone older had been her friend,
advised her, cajoled her –
If only she'd had the strength to quit and the long legs to walk out.
If only if only if only – the sharp edge of "if only"

could literally eviscerate and leave you lonelier than the
mornings when you still shared the bed.

The burnished amber of November leaves caught the late
afternoon sun.
It was an extra-blanket-tonight sort of day, made for looking back
and letting some sweet times in too.
She would call it an early night,
no use burning the candle at both ends.
Maybe it would be a peaceful sleep
without the wakeful dreaming.
Maybe waking would be gentle, hopeful, absent of recrimination.
Maybe just maybe God would grant the grace to accept the
differences.
She closed her eyes in almost-prayer.

COMFORT FOOD

It used to be that comfort
Was tapioca and custard,
A plate of macaroni,
Ham and cheese, a little mustard.

It was sittin' around on Sunday,
Football on the tube,
Mom was doin' laundry,
The truck was gettin' lubed.

But here it is, what it is –
Me hangin' out to dry.
How I got here God only knows
And I'm not even goin' to try.

A drop of this, a patch of that,
That's what they call the comfort pack –
To dull my senses, drown the sorrows
Shorten the count on too many tomorrows.

They want to know do I want the priest?
I try to tell them, "Not in the least!"
The words I need will belong to me.
I'll sing the song that sets me free.

It'll be a simple lulla lulla bye bye –
No wanton sentimental dry cry of
Sweet dreams, peace & love, eternal bliss.
Actually? In reality? It will go like this:

"Just a skip and a jump
On the wing of a prayer
Surely will get me
From here to there.

May mercy and goodness
Surround my bed
May forgiving those trespasses
Ease the pain in my head."

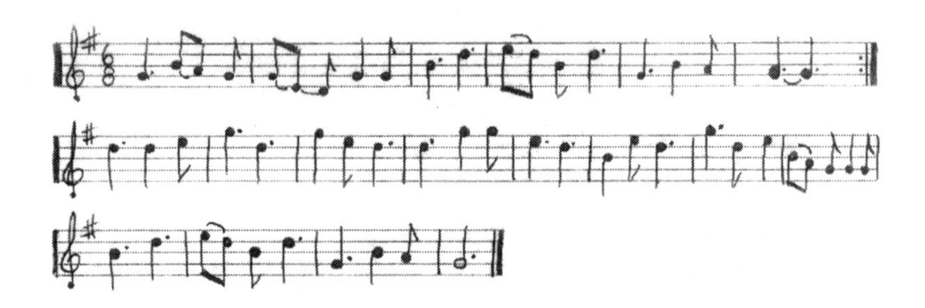

EXTENDED CYCLING

Michael's in Ohio
 His mother's dying in Maine
 He's waiting.
His baby girl is due any moment;
 her mama's bags packed for the hospital;
His open-ended airline tickets sit on the counter.
Imminent, forthcoming, ready.

Michael's sister Kathy
Lives the next town over from Mom,
 manages everything logistical.
Kathy's sister Joanne
Lives close by, stops by in the afternoon to hug her mom.
Joanne's brother Danny
Lives down the pike, can't do the sheet changing
 but helps with the books.
Kathy's second son, Little Danny,
 agreed to move his family into Granny's to help out.
More room than the trailer,
 but more complicated than he ever imagined.
He wishes his three brothers would come over more often.
Lynn waits for Danny to come home, late from work again;
 maybe he can get Alyssa in the tub, help John with his
 homework, or just hold Ava.

Ava's eyes hone in on Granny; her applesauce cheeks grin;
 the banging spoon and toothless song make Granny smile.
Granny just heard Bob – "Jesus Christ, Marilyn,
 what's taking you so long!"
She sees Bob more often, almost every day now he comes to visit.
Bob is Michael & Kathy & Joanne & Danny's father.
He's been gone for 17 years; or has he?

The very day Ava for the very first time
    figured out how to sit up by herself,
Granny lost her ability to sit up by herself.
In the moments when her mind clears,
    Granny marvels at this turn of events.
She contemplates synchronicity and the spokes of her life,
    propped and wedged in her wheel chair, waiting.

THE FURIES

We were born twins, allegedly identical;
but she was the pretty one;
I, always the plain.
From the time we learned to distinguish ourselves
through the words of others, this was so.
Sweeter smiles fell around her and I grew to resent my sister.
As close as we were in flesh and experience, and though I knew
her every move and smell change and roll of the eye
as she did mine,
our heartbeats pounded out of synch.
My mother had to part us, with frequency;
if it wasn't with The Look, the dish towel snapped us into
backing off; she called us her Furies.
"Why?" we whined.
"Because you two are bound to each other with a vengeful love;
in the end, it'll eat you both. Mark my words."
Papa scolded me when he saw envy envelop my being.
"Got the cat scratch fever again, Sissy?
Go to your room and sit it out."
But the tables have turned.
The growths plunging out of her breast, her neck, her stomach
have proven to be the great equalizer.
Drawn, sunken, dry, she can no longer lay sole claim to beauty.
People comment on the smoothness of my skin;
they say I look good for my age.
I turn my head in pleasure. I can't suppress a smile.
I fantasize the reddening, burgeoning tumors
bursting and spewing green metallic slickness;
I can taste it in the back of my throat.
The poison, emanating from our embryonic cauldron,
belongs to me as well as to my sister.
The first whiff of her rot did not repulse me;

I sensed her pain before she dared admit to it;
Secretly I mouthed,"You get what you deserve."
I wished for her death and continued to celebrate
 Christmas and Easter and birthdays.

Now, I change her dressings every day;
 soft cloths swab her seeping wounds.
My hands caress the skeleton I once curled around in our womb
 as fear grips the depth of my organs. When her eyes find mine
 she is both pleading and sardonic but the cat's got her tongue–
I too have no words.
I am made weak by the waves that course through us.
Is my venom her ravaged body?
Was my mother right about us?
Friends marvel at our close relationship and assure me that our
 love for each other will endure through thick and thin. Some
 people don't know when to shut up.
Surrounded by the menagerie of her family,
 my sister is dead set against dying.
People say she is waiting for reconciliation with her pitiful son.
Our sisters promise her the Kingdom of Heaven
 with Mama and Papa just around the corner,
 while her quarrelsome daughters beg her not to leave them.
The hang-dog boyfriend bends to her every gesture.
I should be grateful for his help.
I should go to confession to cleanse.
I should apologize to my sister.
"Margaret, I'm sorry."
Maybe she will apologize to me.
"Eleanor, I'm sorry."
One of these days, as the shroud hovers, the storm cloud
 will cover our impending, heart-wrenching split.

MAKING NICE

The social worker tells me
"Forgive your dad before he dies."
A part of me agrees with her,
but my memory hopes he fries.

How to erase the years when
negligence had no measure –
How to suddenly embrace
the ogre as a treasure.

Who's the grown up now?
And who's become the child?
Who gives, who takes the care
without either being defiled?

DECISION

It was a good decision
Now and then
So why do I feel
Like a rat in a pen?

Impossible questions, feelings confounding
Querulous answers, issues compounding
I'm left alone by my sisters and brother
To calculate interest I pay to my mother

Carrying no longer the weight of her breath
I wait at a distance for the tidings of death
When I gave up the daily giving of care
I traded for a heaviness that's harder to bear

I am plagued to this day
I have to say
With guilt – gnawing and rasping
At 3 AM it leaves me gasping

The guilt is not about making the decision
There is no need for taking back or revision
It's that *more* than sadness or impending grief
I feel such wonderful sweet relief

MARRIED LIFE

I see him framed
through the door jam
standing in the dining area,
rifling the cupboards for snacks –
undoubtedly Oreos, maybe even fig newtons.
He seems miles away and as if in a moving picture,
a foreign film, untranslatable.
He rifles and he paces with purpose,
gleeful when he finds an open package of something.
She sits at a table, hands in her lap watching him,
perhaps hoping he will find her a snack as well.
With a kiss to her forehead he sits down beside her.
The aides tell me they get cozier every day.
He's even found her room.
She discovered his many weeks ago.
They are delicate and innocent with each other –
really quite tender –
I turn away.

Who would ever guess that I have been married to him for 49 years –
that we have children and grandchildren – that I still dust his desk?
Certainly not he;
Most certainly not she.
I remember the first time he kissed me.
He asks me each day I come, "Just who are you exactly? Do I
know you?" By the time he actually dies, he will have left me
more than once. There will be a day, soon, when I can no
longer stand here watching. There's no tear of jealousy.

Things being what they are I am glad for their shared human
kindness, but the loss of any thread of us makes me too sad
to be the spectator.

IT'S NOT RIGHT

I got a phone call last night;
My son died.
He was 75.

My niece says he broke his hip a few weeks back, laid in bed,
wouldn't do his exercises.
Ended up not caring.
I think he did himself in;
don't know exactly how.
Sure glad my wife wasn't here for this news;
it would've killed her.
It's not right to have your child die before you.
It's not the way it's supposed to be –
not in the natural order of things.
I've seen everything now;
I guess I've lived too long.

PILLOW TALK

You heard of those nursing home cats?
They mystery walk the halls
settlin' in rooms of folks next in line in the dyin' parade.
Nurses say these cats are good at their predilections –
On the money by a day or two –
"There goes the cat – so goes Mrs. So & So."

Thelma and Lil Bit were somewhat like that but different too.
Silken softness was Lil Bit,
Gray fur not too short, not too long.
The runt of the litter who found Thelma's doorstep the day
Thelma's doctor found the cancer.
She asked for extra feedin'at the beginnin' –
That grew into extra love, givin' back each nibblet times two.
Even more as Thelma got sick, then sicker.
That Lil Bit;
She would settle in right up around Thelma's head,
Tail fanning down around Thelma's neck.
You could barely see the pillow.
"My feline halo," Thelma used to say;
"She fixes my pain better than the morphine.
Takin' me home she is."

The day Thelma left, the cat left too.
Thelma's heart was beatin' and she was breathin' irregular like
with big spaces in between.
"Soon," they said.
But we knew Thelma, and I'm tellin you she was already dead.
"She ain't here no more," we told 'em.

That Lil Bit just plain, outright disappeared – Whoosh! Gone!
Vamoose!
After a day or two, Thelma's body finally stopped.

We put food out for the cat for a couple of weeks.
We called her, we left the back porch screen open a notch,
    but still no sign.
A coyote most likely took her on home.

INTO THE TWILIGHT

These days, I am a Twilight Miss, wrapping The Veil around and around my wavering bones, gliding down the stony riverbed.
I let my toes get wet and I dance the tango. Beauty surrounds me.

The other day, I went to the chapel; I took my ticket;
I called out my name announcing that I had come –
"Glenna Blaisdell here."
But they didn't take me.
I heard friendly voices but those voices weren't shaping my name.
It must not have been my turn –
 or else they didn't hear me.
At this moment, I'm afraid of the moment that's approaching
 and I cannot pin down the moment that just was.
I see only sparkles on the ceiling; if I stop moving my lips,
 my silence softens my racing heart.
When it's my time I better not putter and splutter around –
 that's not like me – I'm not one to dillydally.
 I get right down to business.

Besides: I've done all I could do.
What more is there? Right?

I remain the survivor, but maybe I am losing my get up and go.

I am becoming the Twilight Mist – fine droplets of cloud
 prism my splintering soul into finely cut crystal to be placed
 gingerly on the top shelf catching afternoon sunrays and
 specks of dust from the sweeping.

Ahh.......

I don't think God's forgotten me.

NOW THAT'S DENIAL

They moved up from the city to live on an island –
Isolated but free from constraint, way off the grid,
lit by the sun, inspired by the tilt of the windmill.

With the requisite chickens, the occasional hog,
the summer berries, the harvest plenty,
Life was not canned, it was preserved.
The trips to the mainland were regular but not frequent,
planned and executed with forethought and thrift –
Smooth sailing, no careless drift.

It was noted some years back that a strange strawberry appeared
on his neck but decades of living had taught them to expect
anomaly, to incorporate the four leaf clover as a normal and
welcome addition to the variety of bloom in their environs.
They also observed the growth confidently enlarging, the reddish–
pink hue burning more brightly with time.
Ah, age spots and wens, skin flaps and failing eyesight –
The price of getting on.

"Perhaps we should get this checked out," she said as the walnut
size bulge became a golf ball.
"What do they know?" he said. "I am fine."
The seasons changed again and again, and the golf ball protruded,
even itched, sometimes got in the way of buttoning down his
collar against the wind, and gradually morphed into an orange,
a blood orange from some exotic orchard.
"It doesn't look good," she said –
when an ooze began staining his shirts.
One day, around the time of a scheduled trip to the mainland,
there was a bursting and expulsion – the center did not hold.
She soaked three kitchen towels and said, more firmly this time,
"We need to ask a doctor."

"What do you think they will do except take our money? We
should use the hot soaks. I'll drain it myself if it comes to that."

They went to the mainland.
They saw a doctor.
Tests were taken –
scans and blood draws, tissue biopsies and scopes.
"There is cancer in your throat, in your jaw, down your esophagus,"
said the doctor.
"Oh no," she said.
"Can't be," he said. "You've made a mistake. You've put my name
on somebody else's pictures."

They went back to their island despite the choppy seas
and ominous wind that blew that day.
"Imagine that," he said. "We went through all that falderol,
and some poor fellow will be thinking he has a clean bill of
health just because they can't keep things straight."

"Oh, you know them," she said. "They think they know it all."

PERPLEXING PROGNOSIS

How in the world does she keep going?
There is nothing clinical to support her existence.
Skeletal doesn't begin to describe the form
that curls into the pillow.
Intake? Nothing. Accepts sips of fluid but hasn't eaten in a month.
Output? Almost nothing. Sometimes muddy, clear just as often.
Her heart rate paints images of turtles.
There are no longer any relevant measures.

I deemed her imminently dying three months ago.
I readied the family; they started calling the cousins.
After a day or two, she miraculously rebounded;
I was met with bright eyes and intelligible speech.
With the second and third phoenix impersonations,
I started questioning my skills of prognostication.
The woman induces me to shrug,
to raise my eyebrows, to shake my head.

She declared the other day, while I attempted to find her vitals,
that despite various welcoming salvos from the other side,
she found herself lost;
she just didn't know how to get there from here.
I questioned the cosmic mapquest:
What indicators am I to chart?
No one answered me. Oz was apparently on coffee break.

I will have to reconcile myself to the not knowing.
I am supposed to know, to have the answers;
If the doctor writes it, then it's so.
But she's unwinding at her own pace and I have no choice
but to diagnose a classic case of the dwindles;
For all I know, she's living on motes of dust.

THE COLORS OF DYING

I see me in the mirror of my mind.
I am Dusky
I am Waxy
I am Mottled.
Blotchy pools of purple oozing into
A grayer shade of gray.
My heart must be triaging – letting my toes know their jig is up;
dancing days are done yet Twitch and Flinch
volunteer my body to do their bidding.
They call me Imminent
They say I'm Active
I Empty out but am Filling up – there is no void
Just transition

I agitate I cogitate I regurgitate one being into another sphere.
I see the liquid coming toward me through a slit in my face
but I cannot know where my mouth has gone.
She say shh she say shhh shh she say
I say Country hoe – gimme spice
Bring it on it be nice
She say once
I say twice
Shh shh –shh shh shh – shhhhh

TIRED, BONE TIRED

We didn't know it was going to be so hard. We really didn't. On the dignity bandwagon, full of hope, respecting his choice to go at home, we kids conference called and made the decision to bring him back to his retirement nest where he and Mom had been promised 'aging-in-place.' She died in a hospital. The pamphlets hadn't really talked about the end, the real ass end, of life.

All of us were willing; we had supportive and participating partners and our children were nearly adults. Some of us even were medical professionals. We had a leg up on this situation. We used vacation time, blocked out calendars with "going home," "my turn," or just plain "Dad." The doctor had said weeks, a matter of weeks and so we shifted into high gear. All six of us were high functioning Type-A's after all; we would adapt, we could do this for our father. It was a no brainer, straight from the heart. We hunkered down and cut the deck, each taking turns cooking, changing laundry loads, emailing friends and family, scheduling appointments, meds, nurses, each other.

Keeping up with the sheets became our benchmark of success or failure, how we measured each other shift by shift. Despite the pads, those dependable, disposable pads, it was the sheets that started to get the best of us. How soon, it seemed, "we can do this" degenerated into "can we do this?" "You didn't" and "she should have" began creeping into our conversation behind closed doors or even in the driveway.

We began sniping and snarking. Us? Only other people acted this way. Our friends and spouses cleared their throats and rolled their eyes; some brave souls even made helpful suggestions like "What about getting extra help in here?" The morning that I dropped the coffee maker, the toilet overflowed and Dad fell forced us to turn a corner; we were entrenched and there was nowhere to go but deeper.

So we regrouped; we facilitated ourselves into new understanding. Medications were changed. Dad's agitation, at least, was lessened. More vacation time was taken. Blackberries and cell phones were never far away or quiet as we scrambled to pretend we still had our "regular" lives. But we knew as we saw the dark circles widening under our eyes, smelled the acridness of our skin after one of Dad's hard nights that escape from this time warp was delusional, that we were bubble wrapped and free falling. What we didn't know was the meaning of marathon.

The doctors said, "Can't figure it out." The hospice nurses said, "Don't know what's keeping him here." My sister's boss said, "How long is this going to take!" There was no easy calibration of days and hours and minutes; even seconds became universes unto themselves; our movements were lugubrious and slower than slow, yet our minds were feverish; our speech devolved to the level of "see spot run." We danced each intricacy of the day in perfect time and in synch with each of our father's decreasing breaths. We were being kept alive by our dying Daddy.

And then, he died. My brother Tom read to him that night; he told my sister Ann he loved her; he squeezed my hand. We made our makeshift beds and went to sleep. And then, he died. We woke up the next morning to a new world – not shocking but still strangely unexpected. We huddled on the couch, small children again, and exhausted, spent as if we had never slept; we couldn't lift our limbs, we could barely breathe. Our morning mouths were stuck with night scum. Finally, my brother said, "We should call everyone." We didn't move, waiting for infinity to pass.

WITH A FLIP OF THE SWITCH

I climb
To the top of the stairs
And stop
Dead in my tracks.
The switch is right here; I know it so well.
After all, how many times have I wiped it clean!
But he was always the one to close up for the night –
bank the fire, lock the door, turn out the hallway light.
"Shutting down now, Mother" and I was there
turning down the bed.
All those years...
All those years, he was such a stickler for making a tight house.
Prided himself on keeping us safe, he did.
"A man's home is his castle," he'd say.
"A man's duty and place on the earth is keeping his family out of
harm's way," he'd say.

So who's supposed to do that now?
Me, I guess.
It's not that I can't, or that I won't.
It's just that his final shutting down brought about a darkness
that won't ever light up again
no matter how many times I flip that darn switch.

Every once in a while though I can feel him like a flicker,
a filament of light, a whisper of embrace:
"Come on, Mother – one step at a time."

PUDDLING ALONG

At least I'm not flooded with tears every day;
I haven't totally drowned
in the sad waves that wash over me.

I go along doing fine for a few days telling myself,
"Oh, it's not so bad."
"Today, it's not so bad."
Then whoosh – I'm crying in the supermarket, bawling on the highway, absolutely blubbering in the shower.
It was almost easier right after he died.
I was so busy with the arrangements, the paperwork, the lawyer, people calling, the kids hovering, cards in the mailbox.
And all those casseroles!
I sure didn't have any chance to go hungry,
but I haven't been hungry anyway, not really.
It's strange what ends up comforting you.
I've found myself drinking a lot of tea, good old black tea,
a little milk, a sugar or two.
I'm glad for my gardens, I'm glad for my cats,
I'm glad for my cup of tea.

It was hard writing that obituary, believe me.
What's to say about a life?
What's important to tell?
What's interesting?
What's anybody's business?
"Walter McKinnon was a nice guy" – *usually*
"Walter McKinnon was a hard worker" – *when he had to be*
"Walter McKinnon was a great dad" – *most days*
"Walter McKinnon was my love" – *always:*
forget that to death do us part garbage – always is always.

I've started putting the furniture back
   and am contemplating getting rid of the recliner.
I never really liked it, so why keep it now?
It was Walter's cozy spot for years, but the hours, days and weeks
   of sickness in that thing, before the hospital bed took its place,
   is not the picture of Walter I want to remember.
I want to hold on to the good times.
My friend Doris says I should be giving his clothes away, right
   now; somebody else could use them! Well, you know what
   Doris? I can't. I just can't. The recliner is one thing. His plaid
   flannel shirts are another.

Enough of this – the tears are welling up.
I better go put the kettle on.

AFTER THE FACT

There is research;
There are theories;
Books, articles published;
Seminars, workshops attended.

Bereavement is A Topic with Indicators and Risk Factors.
Experts parse, delineating the stages of grief,
the tasks of mourning,
the characteristics and styles of The Grievers.
Studies show that the graphic curve of yearning,
drawn from the revelations of the longest of nights,
trumps disbelief,
anger and even depression in its ascent,
its peaking,
and its rounding down the backside of the bend.
Research subjects are observed for signs of pining away that
exceed predictive, normal limits.

Losing her edges, balance foregone
Slightly myopic but straining to see into beyond
The seamstress fastens the adjusted garment on the mannequin
who used to be her love
now so morphed and transfigured in her mind
that she scrambles the days and months and even years.
Longing, prodded by the short end of the stick,
wandering through grocery store aisles,
guided by insatiable hunger
and driven by blind desire,
she wonders how acceptance is supposed to fit.
Her fingers ache to touch that which is forever
Just beyond reach.

In this state of deprivation what is heard?

The ring of authority proclaiming new findings on measurable
adverse psychological responses? or
the timeless hissing refrain of *Missing You*, a song so old that
identifying original authorship is impossible –
that quantifying frequency, duration and intensity of the singing
sorely tests theories of wave motion and quantum leaps?

In the swale of frailty and the mutability of human sadness,
knowledge seekers may find it difficult to count on robust metrics.

EMPTY BED

Eileen Murphy was admitted to our facility at least 8 years ago when it was determined that she wasn't safe living alone anymore.
She was 89 years old, ambulatory and in overall good health.
Her children could not take her in.
She did not have the resources for one of those Oriental-rug, pretty-furniture assisted living places.
She did have to sell her house.
Her children didn't want that either.
For months she was sad, cry-silently-at-the-window sad.
"But I haven't lost my marbles," she would say.
"You weren't safe, Eileen. We will keep you safe."
"I didn't burn the house down did I?!" was her retort.

A fellow resident, a gentleman of a certain age, tried for months to be a one-person welcome wagon but to no avail. For all his efforts at gallantry he received a polite nod and pursed lips – certainly, no eye contact or words of encouragement.
Then one day, Eileen donned a colorful scarf on her way to the dining room. She knotted it with a flair. And was that rouge on those high cheek bones or was it just the ever-overheated hallway?
Our eyebrows arched; we flashed looks at each other, but of course zipped any comment we were feeling.
She signed up for Keep Your Balance classes and decorated her walker with bows. This led to Yoga for Strength sessions and requests for flowered sheets.
One of her daughters from away, who called every few weeks, interrogated us about her medications; she felt her mother was "high on something!"
"Yes she seems to be," we answered. "We think she's adjusting."
The gent took his cue and offered to accompany Eileen to the patio; she graciously accepted.

They had a fine time, or so we surmised. We definitely kept a respectful distance. It turned out that Eileen had more than one brightly patterned scarf.

The years began to pass.

Eileen proved to be a great party planner at holiday time and she even organized a few spontaneous, off-season hooplas. That's what she would call her gatherings in the activity room – hooplas. We really got to like her – a lot. She wasn't one of the ornery ones. She thanked us for giving her showers. She was polite about the mediocre food. She knew when one of us was having a bad day. She got to recognize other residents' families and made pleasantries. She was fun. She was funny. I looked forward to seeing her when my shift started, to hear how her night was, if her arthritis was getting to her, tidbits of gossip she had picked up since yesterday.

Eileen's decline started, I think, when she was transferred into a double room. Her daughter said funds for a single were running out. She went through a couple of roommates – sharing dreams and groans and moans and stomach rumbles and mutterings and sour air and dying. And then she took a fall, reaching for the walker but with one slippery foot sliding out from under her. We called her children. They came in, paid their respects, stayed for a bit, talked to the administrator, said they'd be back. Eileen turned her head into the wall. One grandchild painted her Grammy a beautiful sunflower for the wall.

"I love you, Grammy."
"I love you too, sweet girl."
"I'll be back, Grammy."
"I hope so, sweet girl."

As fall that year was creeping into the air, Eileen started with that far away stare, then the bouts of pneumonia and UTI's, then the lack of appetite, the weight loss, the overall weakness. We all felt a familiar heaviness coming upon us. How many times we have seen this is beyond calculation. What difference does it make to know the exact number of folks we have seen come and go? After all, we aren't on the bean-counting end of this endeavor. Eileen had entered our hearts beyond professional commitment. We loved her and she had become a precious part of our collective life.

I knew the morning was coming when I would come into work and her bed would be empty, and just around Halloween, after her granddaughter had brought in a glorious orange pumpkin painting, I came into work and her bed was empty. My knees literally buckled. She had gone in the night, between shift changes. The funeral home had already taken her away. Housecleaning was pushing their carts into the room. Room 128, facing east, welcoming the autumn sunrise.

Helen, Eileen's current roommate was craning to catch the action, querulous and curious, the last one to have heard Eileen breathe.

"Is she gone yet? Is she gone yet? Have they taken her?"

One by one, under instruction from no one except our hurting hearts, we began gathering around Eileen's bed. We helped housekeeping strip the bed and wipe down the furniture; we opened drawers and pulled out her scarves, wrapping those rose-scented silk streamers around ourselves and continuing to pack up the rest of the "personal belongings." Such a dull thud descended upon us as we wiped away the salty wetness on our cheeks, readying ourselves for another workday – bathing, feeding, toileting, lifting, cajoling, directing, entertaining over and over and over again on all three floors.

We all had something to say, but no real time to say it all.

"Do you remember the day when...."

"I hope she was peaceful."

"It was great knowing you, dear lady."

Goodbye Eileen –

ABOUT THE AUTHOR

Caroline Macdonald was born in Bellingham, Washington. She graduated from Radcliffe College in 1968.

She and her husband have lived in York, Maine since 1982, and raised three children there. She has worked in hospice in Maine and New Hampshire in the last decade in volunteer management and bereavement support.

Caroline loves to sing while driving, and enjoys long walks on the beach. She is also a journeyman snow shoveler and a *Jedi* master with a wood-splitting maul.

CPSIA information can be obtained at www.ICGtesting.com
Printed in the USA
LVOW10s1254240116

472053LV00022B/1155/P

9 781630 290436